ALL ABOUT

The
Moon
Landing

Chris Edwards

BLUE
RIVER
PRESS

Indianapolis, Indiana

All About the Moon Landing
Copyright © 2023 Blue River Press

Published by Blue River Press
Indianapolis, Indiana
www.brpressbooks.com

Distributed by Cardinal Publishers Group
A Tom Doherty Company, Inc.
www.cardinalpub.com

ISBN: 978-1-68157-139-3
LCCN: 2019957299

Cover Design: David Miles
Book Design: Rick Korab, Korab Company Design
Cover Artist: David Frohbieter
Editors: Dani McCormick, Tessa Schmitt
Illustrator: Amber Calderon
Select Maps: Stefanie Geyer
Images on pages 93, 94, 97, 98, 101, 102, 103 courtesy of
NASA

Printed in the United States of America

10 9 8 7 6 5 4 3 2 1   23 24 25 26 27 28 29 30 31 32

CONTENTS

ALL ABOUT

The Moon Landing

When the *Apollo 11* lunar module *Eagle* landed on the Moon on July 20, 1969, much of the world saw it as a great triumph for humanity and science. For the United States, the Moon landing represented a victory in the space race against the Soviet Union. It provided a positive achievement during a time when Americans were divided over civil rights issues and the Vietnam War. The 1969 Moon landing became an event that united the world for a short time. It showed what could be accomplished through hard work, bravery, and the power of science.

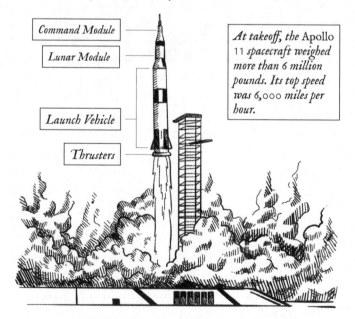

Command Module

Lunar Module

Launch Vehicle

Thrusters

At takeoff, the Apollo 11 *spacecraft weighed more than 6 million pounds. Its top speed was 6,000 miles per hour.*

Yet, the American mission to the Moon had a dark side. With the Moon landing, America was showing their enemy, the Soviet Union, just how far and how accurately the US could shoot a rocket. The United States and the Soviet Union were in a "space race" to see who could put a person on the Moon first and, at the same time, an "arms race" to see who could create the most powerful weapons.

In 2017, NASA was given $19.5 billion in funding to get humans to Mars by 2035.

NASA's Vehicle Assembly Building (part of the Kennedy Space Center)

CHAPTER ONE

The Space Race

The Soviet Union started to arise during World War One (WWI) in the year 1917. A revolutionary group known as the Bolsheviks took power during the chaos that followed Tsar Nicholas II giving up power.

Map of Europe after World War I

Illustration by Stefanie Geyer

Joseph Stalin shakes hands with Joachim von Ribbentrop, the German Foreign Minister, after the Molotov-Ribbentrop Pact is signed.

The Bolsheviks were led by Vladimir Lenin, who created a new government in Russia and founded the Communist Party of the Soviet Union. When Lenin died in 1924, Joseph Stalin took power and became a dictator. Under Stalin, Russia became the dominant country in an empire called the Soviet Union. The Soviet Union took over neighboring countries and spread communism throughout the empire.

In 1933, Adolf Hitler and the Nazi political party

rose to power in Germany. Like Stalin, Hitler became a dictator. Hitler and the Nazis wanted to create a new world and saw Jewish people and the Soviet Union as their major enemies. However, Germany agreed to a 10-year non-aggression treaty with the Soviet Union called the Molotov-Ribbentrop Pact. It was signed on August 23, 1939, allowing both parties to expand without the threat of each other.

By the summer of 1940, the Nazis had taken over much of Europe, including France. Only the British had not been defeated, and they refused to surrender. Germany was more interested in defeating the Soviet Union than beating England. Hitler worried that if Germany did not attack the Soviets quickly, then the Soviets would attack Germany. He began planning Operation Barbarossa, and in June of 1941, Hitler was ready to attack. More than three million German and Axis soldiers invaded the Soviet Union and the Molotov-Ribbentrop Pact was officially broken.

The German army won all of the early battles but stalled outside of two major Soviet cities that winter. These cities were called Leningrad and Moscow.

President Franklin Delano Roosevelt referred to the attack on Pearl Harbor as "a date which will live in infamy."

Moscow was the Soviet capitol and Stalin and the Soviet government resided in the city. In December of 1941, bitterly cold weather froze the German army just outside of these two major cities.

At almost the same time that the German army stalled in the Soviet Union, the Japanese began planning a sneak attack against the United States. Germany and Japan were allies, but the Japanese and Germans rarely communicated with each other. Germany did not know that Japan was planning an attack.

On December 7, 1941, Japanese airplanes bombed an American naval base in Pearl Harbor,

Hawaii. Hitler was upset that the United States had been helping the British and the Soviets with money, food, and weapons, so he used this opportunity to declare war on the United States. The United States government, led by President Franklin Delano Roosevelt (FDR), quickly declared war on both Germany and Japan.

At this point, the United States and Soviet Union were allies against the Nazis, but neither the Americans nor the Soviets thought this alliance would last long. In 1942 and 1943, the Soviet military, known as the Red Army, beat the German army at the Battle of Stalingrad. From that point forward, the Red Army moved toward the German capital of Berlin.

The United States Navy and Marine Corps began making plans to try and win a victory against Germany. General Dwight D. Eisenhower and the British army developed a plan called Operation Overlord. The plan included landing American, Canadian, and British troops, along with other allied forces, on the northern coast of France to drive the Nazis out of France. The invasion, now known as

During the invasion's first day, allied forces had only 132,715 troops in Normandy against Germany's 850,000 awaiting soldiers. Despite the uneven number of soldiers, it was a decisive victory for allied forces.

D-Day invasion, happened on June 6, 1944 and was a success.

After the D-Day invasion, US troops moved east towards Berlin where Hitler and his staff hid in an underground bunker. At the same time, Soviet troops moved west towards the same city. Nazi scientists had just developed an explosive rocket called the V-2, but there was not enough time or money to create enough of these rockets to affect the outcome of the war.

Faced with having to surrender, Adolf Hitler committed suicide on April 30, 1945. Germany surrendered soon after that, and Europe was suddenly divided into two major political areas: East and West. The Soviet army was spread out all over Eastern Europe, and the American army dominated Western Europe.

Germany had surrendered, but Japan had not.

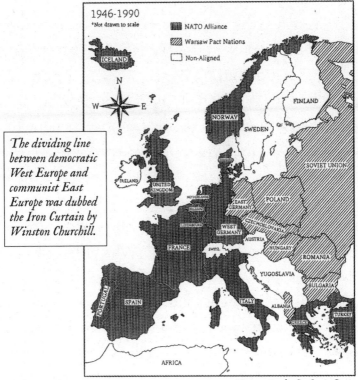

1946-1990
*Not drawn to scale

▓ NATO Alliance
▨ Warsaw Pact Nations
☐ Non-Aligned

ICELAND

NORWAY
SWEDEN
FINLAND
SOVIET UNION

IRELAND
UNITED KINGDOM
NETHERLANDS
BELGIUM
LUXEMBOURG
EAST GERMANY
POLAND
CZECHOSLOVAKIA
WEST GERMANY
AUSTRIA
HUNGARY
FRANCE
SWITZ.
ROMANIA
YUGOSLAVIA
BULGARIA
PORTUGAL
SPAIN
ITALY
ALBANIA
GREECE
TURKEY

AFRICA

The dividing line between democratic West Europe and communist East Europe was dubbed the Iron Curtain by Winston Churchill.

Illustration by Stefanie Geyer

Scientists in the United States worked quickly to make a new super weapon that could help win the war. This super weapon was based on new theories in physics. Between 1905 and 1915, Albert Einstein proved that energy and mass are mathematically equivalent ($E=MC^2$). This meant that energy could suddenly be released from mass under the right conditions.

Earlier, when the Nazis began to take over Eastern Europe, FDR approved the Manhattan Project. The goal of the Manhattan Project was to create an atomic bomb (sometimes called a nuclear bomb). The atomic bomb was a fission bomb, which meant that it worked when an explosive energy drove the pieces of an atom apart. At a very tiny level, these divisions released the energy that held the atomic structure in place. When that energy releases slowly, it is known as nuclear energy. When that energy releases quickly, it becomes a nuclear explosion.

Only heavy elements can be used to make an atomic explosion. Heavy elements have their protons closely packed together. This allows for the energy that breaks one atom to smash into the next one.

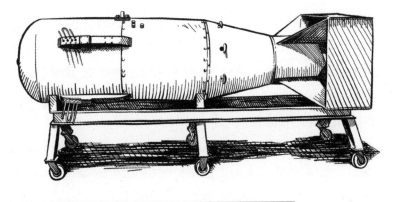

The "Little Boy" bomb was the first nuclear weapon used in warfare when it was dropped on Hiroshima, Japan in 1945.

Uranium was the first natural element used for an atomic explosion, and only a rare version of uranium, which has to be extracted from the metal itself, can be used. The amount of uranium used in the atomic bomb "Little Boy" was about 140 pounds.

FDR died early in his fourth term in April of 1945 and his vice president, Harry S. Truman, took control of the war effort against Japan. Truman urged the Japanese to surrender before they faced total defeat. The Japanese government, led by a young emperor named Hirohito, refused to give up. On August 6, 1945, US bomber Enola Gay dropped an atomic bomb over the Japanese city of Hiroshima. The Japanese still did not surrender. Three days later, the US dropped another bomb on the city of Nagasaki. At the same time, the Soviet Red Army invaded Japanese-held territory in China. The Japanese finally surrendered.

Now that Germany and Japan had been defeated, the United States and the Soviet Union became known as the world's "superpowers." Winston Churchill, a previous British Prime Minister, called the boundary

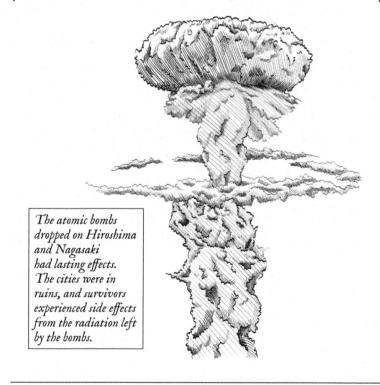

The atomic bombs dropped on Hiroshima and Nagasaki had lasting effects. The cities were in ruins, and survivors experienced side effects from the radiation left by the bombs.

between Eastern and Western Europe an Iron Curtain. Germany was divided into an eastern and western section. Berlin, which was in Soviet-held East Germany, was divided in two. West Berlin was under US control and East Berlin was under Soviet Control.

In 1945, the people of the world had a lot to deal with. The true horror of World War Two (WWII) became apparent as newspapers began reporting about the Holocaust where Nazis murdered European Jews. New threats arose with the building of atomic bombs. And now, the United States and Soviet Union, once allies against Germany and Japan, faced off as enemies.

The *V-2 rocket was the first guided ballistic missile in the world.*

Most of the scientists who worked to create the atom bomb were scared of its power, and some regretted that they had ever built it. However, others now wondered if an atom bomb could be connected to a rocket like the V-2 as a vehicle for delivering a nuclear explosion.

It takes incredible heat and pressure to force hydrogen atoms to fuse together, and when that happens, the process releases energy. This is what the Sun does to produce heat. To understand the process, hold two magnets of the same charge together and they will push away from one another. If you push hard enough, the magnets will come together, and the energy that kept them apart is released. If that is done at a large enough scale, it creates an explosion. The same is true when hydrogen atoms are fused together.

An atom bomb made it possible to create a hydrogen bomb. The V-2 rocket made by German scientists made it possible to put atomic bombs and hydrogen bombs on rockets. After 1945, the United States and the Soviet Union both worked quickly to create as many bombs as they could. The problem was that these bombs were so powerful that a war between the US and Soviet Union would destroy both sides and maybe the whole world.

Each government wanted to show off their ability to shoot long-distance rockets without actually starting a war. The United States and the Soviet Union needed a way to show that they could control space. This was how the space race started, and the ultimate target for a long-distance rocket rose every night right above both the Soviet Union and United States: the Moon.

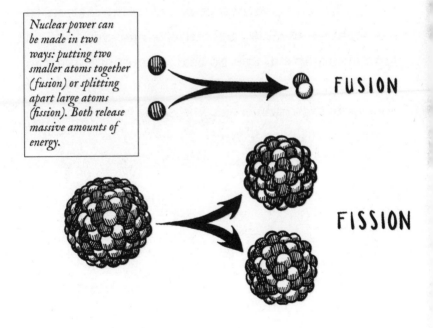

Nuclear power can be made in two ways: putting two smaller atoms together (fusion) or splitting apart large atoms (fission). Both release massive amounts of energy.

FUSION

FISSION

CHAPTER TWO

Sputnik

The United States did not have a lead in the arms race for very long. The Soviets had spies in the US atomic program that sent information to the Soviets. In 1949, the Soviet Union released an atomic bomb in the Soviet country Kazakhstan

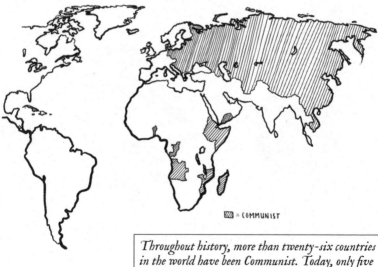

▨ = COMMUNIST

Throughout history, more than twenty-six countries in the world have been Communist. Today, only five countries remain under communist control.

to study its effects. By this time, much of Asia was under a communist government. China had become a communist dictatorship in 1949. The Korean peninsula was divided in half between communism and capitalism.

North Korea was a communist state. The country's dictator was named Kim Il Sung. South Korea was allied with the United States. In 1950, Kim Il Sung ordered his army to invade South Korea. This began the Korean War which lasted from 1950 to 1953. No nuclear weapons were used in the Korean War, and the Soviet Union did not send in the Red Army. The Korean War showed fighting could easily break out between communist and capitalist countries.

At the end of WWII, the United States brought about 1,600 captured German scientists to the US in what was known as Operation Paperclip. One of those German scientists, named Wernher von Braun, had been the man in charge of creating the V-2 rocket for the Nazis. Von Braun now worked for the United States and was told to begin creating a long-range missile.

In 1952, two important discoveries were made. First, the United States military exploded a hydrogen bomb in the Pacific Ocean. A hydrogen bomb explosion is like a little piece of the sun. The nuclear energy of an atomic explosion becomes so hot that it fuses hydrogen. Atom bombs are called fission bombs, because they split atoms apart. Hydrogen bombs are called fusion bombs, because they fuse

Von Braun worked for the United States Army after World War II and developed the rockets used to launch America's first satellite, the Explorer 1.

atoms together. Atom bombs are hot enough to make hydrogen bombs, which is why these bombs are called thermonuclear weapons. They combine nuclear energy with extremely high heat.

Secondly, von Braun wrote that it would be possible to send a rocket into space if the engine was big enough and the fuel was strong enough. The United States government began to see the value in sending rockets into space.

In 1953, the Korean War ended in a draw. The Soviets tested a hydrogen bomb of their own, and it was successful. The United States and the Soviet Union both held bombs with the explosive power of a small sun. The race was on to see who could connect those bombs to rockets that could be sent around the world to hit a target in just a few minutes.

Compared to the Soviet Union, America was more economically stable after WWII. This gave America a lead in the development of the atomic and hydrogen bombs. However, the Soviets had Sergei Korolev, one of the great geniuses of scientific history. Stalin put Korolev in prison and forced the scientist to work while there. Months after Stalin died in 1953, Nikita Khrushchev became the sole leader of the Soviet Union.

Khrushchev put Korolev in charge of the Soviet space program but kept Korolev's name top-secret. The rest of the world would only know that the Soviet space program was led by a chief designer.

Korolev was more interested in space exploration than he was in making weapons. He had taken the

Korolev (above) is thought of by many as the father of astronautics, but his identity was kept a secret until after his death.

designs for the German V-2 rocket and improved upon them to make the R-1 and R-2 rockets. By 1953, the Soviets had built an R-7 rocket based on his design.

The R-7 could launch with a load of more than five tons over a transcontinental distance. It was strong enough to tow an object into space. Then, Korolev used his experience in making rockets and his knowledge of physics to create the first human-made satellite. It would go by the name *Prostreishiy Sputnik*. Translated into English, this means "simple traveling companion." A satellite is an object that is caught in the gravity of a larger object in space. This causes the satellite to orbit, or rotate around, the larger object. For example, the Moon is a satellite of Earth, and continually rotates around the planet.

Back in the late sixteen-hundreds, the English mathematician Isaac Newton proved that the force of gravity gets weaker as an object moves away from the center of Earth. With enough force, an object could escape Earth's gravity and enter into outer space. Mathematically, an object would need to reach a speed of 25,000 miles per hour to hit the escape velocity necessary to leave Earth's gravity.

Korolev knew that a satellite could be put into space and then made to orbit Earth. The R-7 rocket was strong enough to take a satellite into space, and Korolev intended to do this. The Soviets began testing their rockets and in 1955 announced plans to send a Soviet-made satellite into outer space.

On October 4, 1957 the Soviet space program launched an R-7 rocket into space. The satellite *Sputnik* began to orbit Earth. *Sputnik* was not a weapon, but the Soviet government used its achievements to shake the confidence of America. *Sputnik's* successful

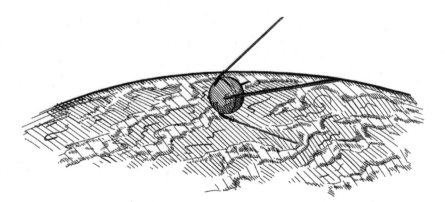

Sputnik *was the first man-made satellite put into orbit around Earth. It fell back to Earth in 1958 and was damaged beyond repair.*

orbit was barely mentioned in the official Soviet newspaper. *Sputnik* was only 22 inches in diameter and made out of aluminum. President Eisenhower, the general who led the D-Day invasion to free France from Germany in 1944, was not worried about *Sputnik*. The American people were amazed and alarmed by the success of *Sputnik*.

By 1957, millions of American households had televisions, and Americans had become used to watching the nightly news. The launch of *Sputnik* made for a popular television news story, because the satellite could be watched as it orbited Earth. Experts used charts to explain the route that *Sputnik* took through space. Newspaper headlines called the Soviet satellite the "Red Moon," because the Soviet flag was red. Anybody in the world who had the right equipment could listen to *Sputnik's* radio signals beeping across the airwaves. In early October of 1957, *Sputnik* seemed to be the only thing that Americans could think about.

Nikita Khrushchev was thrilled to find out that the Americans feared and admired *Sputnik*. He saw an opportunity to show the world that Soviet

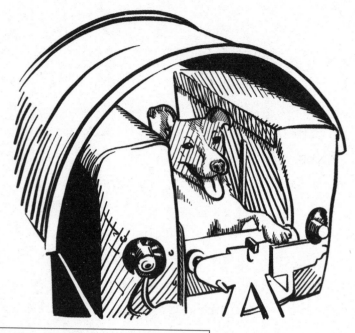

Laika has been honored throughout the world in the form of statues, stamps, and art.

communism was better than American capitalism. He ordered Korolev to make another satellite and start working on plans to put a person into space.

At that time, no one knew if living creatures could survive in space. The Soviets decided to experiment by sending an animal into orbit. About one month after *Sputnik* was sent into space, the Soviets launched *Sputnik 2* with a dog named Laika inside.

Laika proved that a living being could survive a rocket launch. Later into the trip, Laika died, presumably from overheating.

President Eisenhower was not impressed by the *Sputnik* missions. However, he understood how worried many Americans were about the lead that the Soviets had in space exploration. The US tried to launch a satellite, called *Vanguard*, into orbit in December of 1957. The *Vanguard* rocket flew for two seconds before it blew up.

Realizing how far behind the US was, Eisenhower decided to create a new organization that would focus on space travel and exploration. This organization would not be connected to the military. In July of 1958, the National Aeronautics and Space Act was passed. This created the National Aeronautics and Space Agency, known as NASA. NASA became an official US agency on October 1, 1958, almost one year after the first *Sputnik* launch.

Sputnik sent radio signals for about three weeks and continued to orbit until early 1958, when Earth's gravity pulled it into the atmosphere. *Sputnik* burned up in the sky like any ordinary meteor. With NASA in place, the Americans were determined to catch up with Soviet technology. The space race was heating up.

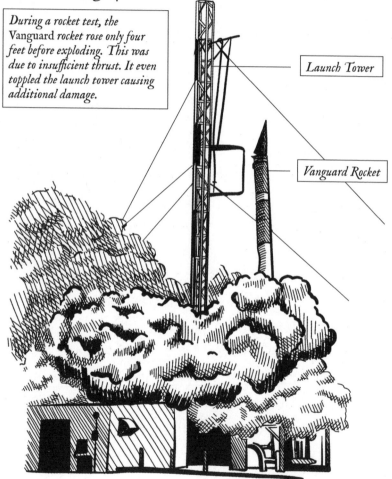

During a rocket test, the Vanguard rocket rose only four feet before exploding. This was due to insufficient thrust. It even toppled the launch tower causing additional damage.

Launch Tower

Vanguard Rocket

CHAPTER THREE

The Chosen Seven

NASA's first act was to send a satellite called *Explorer 1* into space. Eisenhower thought that satellites could be used to spy on the Soviet Union. He also believed that the *Explorer 1* would show the world that the United States could keep up with Soviet space technology.

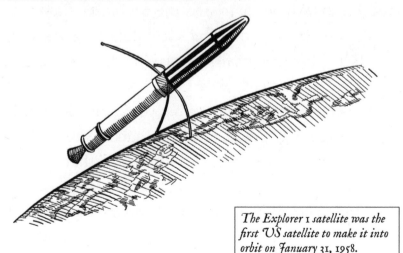

The Explorer 1 satellite was the first US satellite to make it into orbit on January 31, 1958.

Meanwhile, the Soviets sent up the *Sputnik 3* satellite in 1958. Then in 1960, *Sputnik 5* went into a one-day orbit with many living creatures on board. Inside the satellite were fruit flies, plants, forty mice, two rats, a rabbit, and two dogs. All of them came back alive. It seemed possible that a human being could survive a long rocket ride into space.

The *Sputnik* missions were not the only way the Soviets showed off their lead in the space race. On January 2, 1959 the Soviets launched the *Luna 1*. This was an unmanned probe that was supposed to land on the Moon. It missed the Moon by almost 4,000 miles. Even so, the *Luna 1* sent data back to the Soviets and became the first human-made spacecraft in history to completely leave Earth's gravity.

In September of the same year, the Soviets launched *Luna 2*. Soviet scientists had created the *Luna 2* so that it would leave a vapor trail that star-gazers across the world could watch. The *Luna 2* was designed to literally hit the Moon, and after a trip of just over sixty-four hours, it crashed onto the lunar surface.

Strelka and Belka were recovered alive, which made people optimistic that manned spaceflight was possible.

The *Luna 2* was not just a stunt; it sent back scientific data to the Soviet scientists. Because of the *Luna 2*, the Soviets knew that the Moon was not surrounded by magnetic fields or radiation. This was important to know if the Soviets were going to try to put cosmonauts on the Moon.

Just a few weeks after the *Luna 2's* success, the *Luna 3* launched on October 4. This was the most impressive mission yet as the *Luna 3* went around the

Moon to the never-before-seen "dark side" and took pictures from a distance of just over 41,000 miles. When the *Luna 3* got closer to Earth, it sent those pictures back to the Soviets using radio transmitters. Today, any cell phone can send pictures through space, but in 1959, this technology seemed futuristic. The pictures of the dark side were in black-and-white and not very clear, but the Soviets—not the Americans—had taken them.

The Luna 3 *took seventeen usable photos of the far side of the Moon, giving people their first look at that side.*

In the United States, 1960 was a presidential election year. The presidential race featured Dwight Eisenhower's vice-president, Richard Nixon, running against John F. Kennedy (JFK). The election was one of the closest in the nation's history, but JFK won. JFK was only forty-three years old when he became president, which made him the youngest person ever elected into the presidential office. Youthful, handsome, and well-read, he seemed to be the perfect president to lead America into the space age.

By the time JFK took office, NASA had existed for more than two years, but the Soviets were still leading the space race. The chief Soviet designer, Sergei Korolev, led the creation of the *Vostok 1* spacecraft. The *Vostok 1* was a space satellite big enough to hold a human passenger. The Soviets launched the craft into space on April 12, 1961 with a cosmonaut named Yuri Gagarin on board.

Gagarin became the first human in space. The *Vostok 1* went around the Earth one time in a trip that took almost two hours. Earth's gravity then pulled the *Vostok 1* out of orbit and Gagarin ejected himself from the capsule and parachuted safely to the

Gagarin graduated from flight school and went on to be chosen for the Soviet space program in 1960.

ground. This was a huge victory for the Soviet space program.

Nikita Khrushchev, leader of the Soviet Union, was thrilled that the Soviet space program had once again shown up the Americans. He was also excited that a new communist leader, a young lawyer named Fidel Castro, had taken power from a dictator named Batista on the island nation of Cuba.

Cuba was just ninety miles south of the state of Florida. The Soviet Union now had an important ally close to American soil.

As Castro created his government, the Soviets sent another cosmonaut, named Gherman Titov, into space where he went around Earth seventeen times over the course of 25 hours.

The United States was now preparing to respond by sending their astronauts into orbit as a way of matching the Soviet space program. NASA began recruiting some of the best pilots in the US military to be astronauts in the space program.

Illustration by Stefanie Geyer

Cuba allying with the Soviet Union was very concerning to Americans, because Cuba is very close to the continental United States.

NASA wanted military pilots who were under forty years old and less than five feet, eleven inches tall. The astronauts had to be physically fit and small enough to fit in a space capsule. NASA also required that any potential astronaut have a college degree in a scientific field and be a certified pilot with at least 1,500 hours of experience flying jets. After a long screening process where potential astronauts had to be subjected to a series of painful physical exams and tests, seven men were chosen to be the first of America's space explorers.

On April 9, 1959 NASA introduced the seven pilots who would become known as the astronauts. These pilots would become some of the most famous people in the United States. Their names were Alan Shepard Jr. (Navy), Virgil "Gus" Grissom (Air Force), Gordon "Gordo" Cooper (Air Force), Walter "Wally" Schirra (Navy), Donald "Deke" Slayton (Air Force), John Glenn Jr. (Marine Corps), and Scott Carpenter (Navy). These seven astronauts would be a part of what the NASA leaders called Project Mercury. The goal of Project Mercury was to put an astronaut into orbit around Earth.

After their introduction to the public, the seven astronauts were part of a famous press conference. All of the men were married and had children, and they were asked questions about their families and backgrounds. The astronauts answered the questions in different ways. Gus Grissom, a Korean War veteran from a small-town in southern Indiana, was the least talkative.

The original seven astronauts earned an average annual salary of $10,500 in 1958, which is worth more than $100,000 in 2023. Shown as: (back, l to r) Schirra, Carpenter; (Middle, l to r) Shepard, Grissom, Cooper; (front, l to r) Slayton, and Glenn.

Sam was a rhesus macaque, one of thirty-two monkeys in history to go to space.

One reporter asked Gus what the worst part of the astronaut training program had been, and Gus responded that the worst part was the press conference. John Glenn, a marine corps pilot and WWII hero, seemed the most comfortable. Glenn had already been on a TV game show in 1957 called *Name That Tune.* At age thirty-seven, Glenn was the oldest of the astronauts and gave the longest answers to the questions asked.

Before NASA sent any of the Mercury Seven into

space, they sent Sam, a rhesus macaque monkey. Their goal was to test the Mercury space capsule, nicknamed the *Little Joe 2*, and observe the effects of space on human-like beings. Sam did well on the flight, which was encouraging for NASA's aim of sending man to the Moon. As the monkey returned home, it seemed that very little skill would be required to fly a spacecraft. While riding in the space capsule did not require much piloting skill, the astronauts were deeply involved in operating the capsule. In an emergency, they had to be prepared to take control or otherwise risk their safety.

CHAPTER FOUR

Freedom Flight

In May of 1961, Alan Shepard was chosen to be the first American astronaut to be sent into space. Shepard was a WWII veteran and became a naval aviator in 1947. Shepard named his space capsule the *Freedom 7*. The capsule was attached to the nose of a Redstone space rocket. Shepard was supposed to be shot into space where his capsule would detach from the rocket and begin orbiting Earth.

When asked what he would be thinking in the moments before the launch, the astronaut showed quick wit saying, "the fact that every part of this ship was built by the lowest bidder." Shepard's flight would be different from Yuri Gagarin's mission, because Shepard would be able to steer the *Freedom 7* using controls. Gagarin had just been a passenger going for a ride.

NASA's engineers and scientists created a rocket

capable of escaping Earth's gravity, and they built a space capsule that could keep an astronaut alive while he spun around Earth. Yet, no one thought about what to do if Shepard had to go to the bathroom. Outer space is not that far away when you are riding a rocket, so Shepard's journey was only supposed to take about fifteen minutes.

On the day of the launch, however, Shepard got into his spacesuit and was strapped into his capsule. With Shepard strapped in, NASA's engineers began nervously double-checking everything. Almost eight hours went by, and Shepard had to pee. He finally just went in his suit! The urine shorted out the system that was supposed to monitor Shepard's vital signs, but nothing else was bothered.

The first successful human spaceflight by the United States was nicknamed Freedom 7 *by the piloting astronaut, Alan Shepard.*

With tens of millions of Americans watching on television, NASA shot Shepard into space. He went more than one hundred miles into space, but did not orbit Earth. Shepard could not even enjoy a view of space, because the *Freedom 7* had no windows. Instead, Shepard had to watch on a black-and-white screen.

The *Freedom 7* capsule detached from the rocket and was dragged down by Earth's gravity. The heat shields kept the capsule from burning up and a

After a post-flight inspection, Alan Shepard exited the capsule onto the US Navy Carrier Champlain. Outside, he was met by cheers from the surrounding crowd.

parachute slowed the *Freedom 7's* fall. The capsule, with Shepard safely inside, landed near the Bahamas in the Atlantic Ocean and floated until a helicopter came and lifted it back to land. Shepard was the first American astronaut in space.

With Shepard's success, NASA planned to send another astronaut into space. The second Mercury mission would test a craft called the *Liberty Bell 7*. Gus Grissom, the gruff Hoosier, was chosen as the pilot. By this time, many had become accustomed to hearing the success stories of the American and Soviet space programs. However, Grissom's flight would remind people the dangers of space travel.

On July 21, 1961, Grissom was sent into outer space. The *Liberty Bell 7* did not orbit Earth. The capsule simply took Grissom up, then dropped through the atmosphere and into the southern part of the Atlantic Ocean. Everything about the flight had been almost the same as Shepard's flight except that Grissom's space capsule had windows so that he got a better view. The problems began after the flight, when Grissom's capsule landed in the Atlantic Ocean.

The plan was to have the capsule float in the ocean until a military helicopter came and picked it up. The capsules were designed to bob in the water and were air-tight. However, as Grissom was lying in the capsule the side hatch blew off and ocean water started pouring into the capsule. Grissom had to

Landing can be just as nerve racking as lift-off! Grissom's heart rate reached 171 beats per minute as he descended back to Earth.

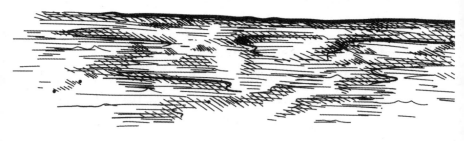

get out fast or he would sink! Luckily, Grissom had inflated a "dam" around the neck of his spacesuit that prevented water from soaking into his suit and sinking him. Gus swam away from the craft and floated in the Atlantic Ocean while the waves bumped him around. He kept an eye out for sharks.

The helicopter that came to retrieve the *Liberty Bell 7* had to give up or risk sinking. The capsule had flooded with too much water and its weight threatened to pull down the helicopter. The helicopter pilot released the cable and the space capsule sank to the bottom of the ocean. Grissom kept floating until another helicopter came and rescued him.

The *Liberty Bell 7* landing was controversial, because some people thought that Grissom had panicked and pulled the lever that burst the hatch. Grissom always denied this. Most technical engineers agree that a malfunction, not Grissom's error, caused the hatch to blow.

John Glenn was charming, patriotic, and married to his childhood sweetheart. The American public tended to think of Glenn as the lead astronaut, but he had not yet been into space. It was now Glenn's turn. In February of 1962, Glenn was sent up into space in a craft called the *Friendship 7*. He became the first American astronaut to orbit Earth. In fact, he took three trips around the planet.

Glenn spent nearly five hours in space, and his capsule came down flawlessly in the Atlantic Ocean. The United States space program, it seemed, had

Although the Navy helicopter tried to save the Liberty Bell 7 *capsule, it was full of water and too heavy to transport. It wasn't recovered until 1999.*

finally caught up with the Soviet Union. Glenn became a national hero, and his space capsule went on a world tour. It seemed the Mercury astronauts could do no wrong.

Those early years of NASA became famous for successes. *LIFE* magazine regularly ran stories on the astronauts and their families. The wives of the astronauts became famous themselves. Reporters liked to interview the wives while their husbands were on dangerous flight missions. Many of the wives had hard lives. They were expected to take care of the household and raise children while their husbands spent countless hours working for NASA. Then, right when they were the most worried about their husbands, reporters would show up with questions and cameras.

In September of 1962, JFK gave what became one of the most famous speeches by any president since Abraham Lincoln's *Gettysburg Address*. President Kennedy delivered his speech at Rice University in Houston, Texas near NASA's Mission Control. Kennedy stated that the United States now had a goal of landing an astronaut on the Moon. The most famous line of the speech was, "We choose to go to the Moon in this decade and do the other things not because they are easy, but because they are hard." Kennedy later proposed working with the Soviet Union towards this goal. NASA's goal was clear; to put an astronaut on the Moon before 1970.

Up until John Glenn's flight, the space race between the Americans and the Soviets had seemed,

Kennedy said that "no single space project in this period will be more impressive to mankind ... and none will be so difficult or expensive to accomplish" as the Moon Landing.

at times, like a harmless competition. The Soviet leader Khrushchev had even given JFK a puppy names Pushinka. She came from the litter of one of the dogs that the Soviets had sent into space.

In October of 1962, things became deadly serious. Launching rockets and satellites into space was something that kept the public's attention, but the real competition between the US and the Soviet Union still involved nuclear missiles.

On October 14, 1962, a US spy plane took pictures of Soviet nuclear missiles being moved into Cuba. Khrushchev had made a new ally with Cuba's dictator, Fidel Castro, and Khrushchev was troubled by the fact that the United States had missiles in Europe. These missiles were close to the Soviet Union and could hit Soviet territory. The Soviets themselves did not have any missiles with the same capacity to hit the United States back. The Soviet missiles in Cuba, however, could cause harm to the US.

President Kennedy made it clear to Khrushchev that the United States would not tolerate the Soviet placement of missiles in Cuba. JFK had to calm several American generals, especially in the Air Force,

Pushinka, meaning "fluffy" in Russian, was the daughter of Soviet space-dog Strelka. After her journey from Russia to the White House, she received her own passport.

who wanted to use the crisis to shoot thermonuclear weapons at the Soviet Union or airstrike Cuba. However, each nation had the capability to destroy the other with nuclear weapons, and Kennedy wasn't ready to risk the well-being of America with a forceful attack.

For thirteen days, Kennedy and Khrushchev had a stand-off regarding the missiles. The entire incident became known as the Cuban Missile Crisis and was probably the closest the world ever came to a full-scale nuclear war.

Khrushchev finally agreed to remove the missiles from Cuba if Kennedy promised to not invade Cuba and remove American missiles from Europe. Kennedy agreed, but the American missile removal was a secret. The Cuban Missile Crisis made Khrushchev look bad to his comrades in the Communist Party, and some of them began to make plans to have Khrushchev removed from power.

Almost a year later, on November 22, 1963, President Kennedy and his wife Jacqueline were riding through the streets of Dallas, Texas in an open-topped car. Crowds lined the street to see the president and first lady. The sound of rifle shots cracked through the air, and JFK slumped over dead.

The American people went into shock when they heard the news. To keep order, Kennedy's vice-president, Lyndon B. Johnson (LBJ) was immediately sworn in as president. Lee Harvey Oswald was soon arrested and accused of having shot Kennedy, but while he was being transported by police, Oswald was shot and killed on live television by Jack Ruby.

Also at this time, the United States was becoming more involved in Vietnam. Communists had taken over northern Vietnam, and the US government was hoping to stop the spread of communism in Asia by preventing the communists from taking over South Vietnam. The Vietnam conflict did not have the same support from Americans that WWII and the Korean War had. The controversy of the war became a central part of American life in the 1960s.

President John F. Kennedy's assassination affected the nation in ways that are still felt today, like the extreme safety measures taken to protect high-profile people.

American social life was also in a process of rapid change. African Americans began to demand their rights. On August 28, 1963 the Reverend Dr. Martin Luther King Jr., along with other public figures, led the March on Washington to the nation's capital. There, in front of the Lincoln Memorial, King delivered his famous "I Have a Dream" speech where he called for racial equality.

Roughly 250,000 people attended the March on Washington to listen to speakers like Dr. Martin Luther King Jr.

Women, too, began to demand a greater place in American life. The Soviets tried to show how they respected women in their society by sending the first female cosmonaut, Valentina Tereshkova, into orbit in 1963 on the *Vostok 6* spacecraft. In 1963, it had been only six years since the launch of the *Sputnik* satellite, but the United States was a very different country than it had been when the space race began.

CHAPTER FIVE

Spacewalk

In 1964, Nikita Khrushchev was removed from power by people high up in the Communist Party. Khrushchev was allowed to retire to a country house while Leonid Brezhnev became the new head of the Soviet Union. Brezhnev continued his support of the Soviet space program. The chief designer Sergei Korolev began to plan a new goal: to have a cosmonaut go on a spacewalk.

A spacewalk would have a cosmonaut float in a spacesuit while connected to the space capsule. The scientific purpose of the spacewalk would be to test if the spacesuits could keep a cosmonaut alive outside of the space capsule, but the Soviet space program also seemed interested in doing something new to show that they were still ahead of NASA.

On March 18, 1965, cosmonauts Alexei Leonov and Pavel Belyayev took off on the *Voskhod 2* spacecraft. On this mission, Leonov exited the spacecraft and floated into outer space. A long cord attached Leonov to the *Voskhod 2*. As Leonov hovered far above the Earth, he began spinning around.

After twelve minutes, he was pulled back to the craft, but his suit was so puffed up from the lack of pressure in space that he could not fit back in. With puffy gloves on, Leonov had to let air out of his suit. This allowed him to slowly move back to the spacecraft, but the physical work caused Leonov to start overheating.

Of being alone in space, Alexei Leonov said, "It was so quiet I could even hear my heart beat... I will never forget that moment."

If Leonov could not make it back into the spacecraft, either because of heat stroke or the changing pressure, then he would die and float in space forever. Luckily, this did not happen. Leonov barely made it back to his spacecraft with the help of Belyayev. The act of floating in space and trying to make it back in while wearing the heavy spacesuit was more difficult than the Soviet scientists had expected.

With Leonov safely inside, the *Voskhod 2* headed back to Earth. The craft suffered serious technical problems that forced the cosmonauts to take over the controls. The *Voskhod 2* landed more than seven hundred miles away from where it was supposed to in one of the coldest places in the world: Siberia. Landing in this remote section of the Soviet Union made it difficult to be found and threatened the health of the cosmonauts. It took two days for the Soviet military to rescue them.

The *Voskhod 2* mission was the last time that the Soviet space program beat NASA at reaching a space milestone. Part of the reason for this was NASA's scientists and engineers had gotten better at designing spacecraft. However, a big reason that the Soviets lost their lead was because their chief designer, Sergei Korolev, died not long after the *Voskhod 2* mission.

Korolev led the Soviet space program for nearly a decade. During that time, he worked long hours despite bad health. His dedication made him valuable to the Soviets. Not only did Korolev work long hours, but he also worried about the cosmonauts who flew the dangerous missions. The Communist Party was very interested in the space program. People high in the government constantly pressured Korolev to do greater and greater things.

All of this wore on Korolev, and by 1966 he was in bad health and needed an operation to remove a growth on his intestine. The Soviet Union's best doctors operated on the chief designer, but during the surgery Korolev died. The Soviet space program would never recover from his death, and soon NASA and the American space program would enter a new era with nine new astronauts.

CHAPTER SIX

The New Nine

After John Glenn's successful flight, it was Scott Carpenter's turn. On May 24, 1962, Carpenter piloted the *Aurora 7* spacecraft. The *Aurora 7* was like a flying lab with several experiments on board, including one that tested how liquid would react in zero gravity. The new information helped NASA prepare for long space voyages, especially when it came to food preparation. Carpenter's craft had several technical problems and landed 250 miles away from where it was supposed to, but Carpenter came home unhurt.

Not long after Carpenter's mission, NASA introduced the "New Nine." These nine astronauts were led by Neil Armstrong, who was one of the world's most gifted and accomplished pilots. The New Nine were supposed to continue working with the original Mercury Seven astronauts, while also leading NASA

The New Nine, the second set of astronauts, became the first group of astronauts with civilian test pilots in the group instead of all military men. Back, l to r: See, McDivitt, Lovell, White, Stafford. Front, l to r: Conrad, Borman, Armstrong, Young

into a new era with the Gemini and Apollo Missions.

The announcement of the New Nine was followed just two weeks later by Wally Schirra's *Sigma 7* flight. By now, spaceflights seemed routine and Schirra came home with plenty of extra fuel. This indicated that a longer flight might be possible. Gordon Cooper then flew the *Faith 7* on May 15, 1963 and came back from space safely. It was time for NASA to do something more challenging.

NASA's first flight director had the name Christopher Columbus Kraft Jr. He worked on the Mercury, Gemini, and Apollo missions and gave out orders like a drill sergeant. Kraft was tough and expected people to listen. Even so, most of the engineers and scientists who worked at Mission Control loved him. If the NASA team was a family, Kraft was the parental -figure. Now that NASA had mastered the art of putting an astronaut into orbit, it was time to give the astronauts more control of the flights.

Christopher Columbus Kraft Jr. was so instrumental in developing Mission Control that NASA later named the building that houses it after him.

Since the Moon's surface was rocky and pitted with craters, a human pilot, not Mission Control, would need to be able to control the spacecraft. This was a hard task as the astronauts would have to navigate the surface, searching for a smooth place to land.

The *Gemini 3* mission would be led by Gus Grissom. On March 23, 1965, Grissom became the first American to go into space twice. Grissom controlled the flight of the craft and changed the degree of the orbit on Gemini's second trip around the Earth, something that had never been done before. Grissom, his crew, and his craft landed safely.

Just a few months later, on June 3, 1965, the *Gemini 4* mission featured the first American spacewalk. Astronaut Ed White floated out into space with a 25-foot cord connecting him to the spacecraft. Oxygen flowed through the cord, and White talked easily with his fellow astronaut, James McDivitt.

White's spacesuit included a camera that allowed him to take what would now be called "selfies" as he floated above the Earth. These images quickly became famous. The whole world could now see what the world looked like from space. White's

Ed White was the first American to walk in space and he took space selfies while doing it! He was awarded the Congressional Space Medal of Honor for his work on Gemini 4.

spacewalk meant that NASA had once again caught up with the Soviet space program's most impressive act. NASA would now look to go beyond the Soviets.

On August 21, 1965, astronauts Pete Conrad and Gordon Cooper were launched into space aboard the *Gemini 5*. The purpose of this mission was to test the ability of astronauts to survive on longer space missions. The Mercury missions had sometimes lasted less than twenty minutes as the astronauts were shot into space only to come quickly back down again. The *Gemini 5* mission was set to last eight full days.

The *Gemini 5* spacecraft suffered some problems with the thruster units and it was hard to keep the power running, yet Cooper and Conrad survived in space for over a week. When they descended back to Earth, their spacecraft landed almost a hundred miles off their target in the Pacific. However, their ability to spend over a week in space made the mission a success. By the end of 1965, the American space program seemed well on its way to achieving JFK's goal of a Moon landing before 1970.

Americans had become used to seeing the footage of NASA on the nightly news. But for many who watched the astronauts, all of whom were white males with crew-cut haircuts, it might have seemed as if they belonged to another era. However, NASA was more integrated than it publicly appeared.

At least four African American women - Mary Jackson, Katherine Johnson, Dorothy Vaughan, and Christine Darden - made important mathematical contributions in NASA. These women, along with many others, were referred to as "human computers." Their responsibility was to solve critical mathematical problems to support NASA's mission. Even as computers evolved through the 1960s and 1970s, human computers were heavily relied on, as their accuracy was unmatched and highly trusted.

The legacy of these women is still felt today as they changed science and the culture of NASA forever.

Many women worked behind-the-scenes at NASA, including (left to right) Mary Jackson, Dorothy Vaughan, and Katherine Johnson.

CHAPTER SEVEN

Turbulent Times

President Lyndon B. Johnson (LBJ) had been elected as president in 1964, and the tall Texan was intent to see civil rights legislation passed through Congress. African American leaders, including Dr. Martin Luther King Jr., demanded change. As LBJ worked to create social change in the United States, he also sent more and more troops into Vietnam.

The Vietnam War went on and on. Starting at age 18, young men had to sign up to be drafted. Only college students did not have to go into the military. The war and the draft caused a lot of anger and arguments in the US. Average Americans could now see images of war on nightly television news broadcasts. Anti-war protests became common across the country, especially on college campuses. The Vietnam conflict seemed very different from World War II, or even the Korean War. LBJ struggled to explain why the US wasn't ending its involvement in Vietnam.

NASA's missions took on a new importance. At a time when the US seemed to have no clear goals in Vietnam, NASA's goal was clear. They wanted to put an astronaut on the Moon. NASA's success gave many Americans something to feel good about at a time when the country was facing massive change and Americans were divided.

The new faces of NASA were Neil Armstrong and Edwin "Buzz" Aldrin. Both Neil and Buzz had served as fighter pilots in the Korean War. Neil Armstrong flew seventy-eight missions in Korea. After the war, Neil enrolled at Purdue University in Indiana, the same school that Gus Grissom attended. He soon earned a bachelor's degree in aeronautical engineering and then became a test pilot. At the time, many astronauts were first test pilots, and Neil decided to follow that path.

Buzz got his nickname as a child when a sibling pronounced "brother" as "buzzer." Over time, the name stuck. Aldrin was a graduate of West Point in New York, which is the Army's college for officer

President Lyndon B. Johnson served in the Naval Reserve during World War II, so he didn't take war lightly, but the Vietnam War was a difficult situation because of the fear of communism spreading.

education. Aldrin became a fighter pilot for the army and flew sixty-six missions in Korea. Instead of becoming a test pilot after the war, Aldrin enrolled at the Massachusetts Institute of Technology (MIT).

Aldrin earned a doctorate degree at MIT by writing his dissertation on the topic of spaceflight. His thesis was so brilliant that NASA's engineers used it as they created the Apollo space program. Aldrin was invited into the astronaut program as a result. Of all the astronauts, Aldrin reached the highest education level. Aldrin was also the most accomplished mathematician of all those put into space.

Buzz Aldrin was sent into space on November 11, 1966 on the *Gemini 12* spacecraft. The commander of that craft was named Jim Lovell. He and Aldrin were going to try and dock the *Gemini 12* with an orbiting rocket, called the Agena, while in space. Aldrin would then spacewalk outside the craft and perform data-collection duties. "Docking" or "parking" a spacecraft would be an important part of any Moon landing, because a Moon landing would require a lunar module (LM) to break away to go down to the Moon. Afterwards, it would have to reconnect with a command module (CM) while in space.

As the *Gemini 12* got closer to docking, the radar system broke down. This meant that the *Gemini 12's* computer system could not regulate speed and distance to make the dock a success. Aldrin's education in mathematics enabled him to figure out the necessary speed and distances. The *Gemini 12* made a successful dock with the Agena rocket. In Buzz Aldrin, NASA had a gifted pilot with the academic skills of a Mission Control engineer.

The NASA Mercury and Gemini missions had been successful, so it was time to move on to the Apollo missions. The Apollo missions would use all of the data and technology from the earlier spaceflights to finally put a person on the Moon. All of the successful missions had blinded many of NASA's engineers to just how dangerous space travel could be. The Apollo missions would begin with a tragedy.

Before taking his first steps on the Moon, Buzz Aldrin decided to take communion, a Christian ritual of eating bread and drinking wine. He encouraged others to give thanks in their own way for this monumental moment.

The Apollo 1 *fire was a huge catastrophe and led to an intense investigation into the cause of the fire and the astronauts' deaths.*

Gus Grissom, one of the original seven Mercury astronauts, was to lead a crew that included Ed White and Roger B. Chaffee. The *Apollo 1* spacecraft was supposed to just orbit Earth as a way of testing Apollo's new technical systems. NASA still believed that the Soviet space program might be the first to the Moon, and so the creation of the *Apollo 1* was rushed. The cabin was filled with almost pure oxygen. Electrical cords tangled on the floor. *Apollo 1* was scheduled to take flight on February 21, 1967, but it never achieved lift off.

After they were bolted into the hatch, a fire broke out when one of the electrical cords became frayed. Since the cabin was filled with pure oxygen, the fire burned out of control. The astronauts did not have time to remove the heavy bolts on the hatch that kept them in. The fire quickly burned up all of the oxygen, and all three astronauts choked to death on the smoke. The Apollo tragedy shook the United States to its core.

At this time, the United States was in upheaval. The Civil Rights Act, passed in 1964, made discrimination based on race illegal. Yet protests continued throughout the country as African Americans and supporters of civil rights continued to fight for racial equality. By 1967, the war in Vietnam had become so controversial that LBJ began to think that he could not win another presidential election.

On March 31, 1968 President LBJ announced that he would not try to run again for the presidency. Five days later, on April 4, 1968, Dr. Martin Luther King

Jr. was assassinated outside of a motel in Memphis, Tennessee. The gunman was an ex-convict named James Earl Ray. Riots and protests broke out across the country. JFK's brother, Robert F. Kennedy (RFK), was in Indianapolis at the time and gave a speech

Robert F. Kennedy told listeners to "...make an effort, as Martin Luther King did, to understand and to comprehend, and to replace that violence...with an effort to understand with compassion and love."

in honor of King to help prevent riots from breaking out in Indiana's capital city.

Nixon promised "peace with honor" in the Vietnam War abroad and a decreased crime rate domestically.

RFK had served as the attorney general of the United States from 1961 to 1964 and had been elected as a senator from the state of New York in 1965. RFK was running for the Democratic nomination for the presidency, and likely would have won, but he was shot and killed on June 5, 1968.

In November of 1968, Richard Milhous Nixon beat former vice president Hubert Humphrey for the presidency of the United States. Richard Nixon had lost to JFK in the 1960 presidential election, but he would now be the man to see JFK's vision of a Moon landing become a reality.

CHAPTER EIGHT

A Man on the Moon

The Soviet space program kept going on after the death of their grand designer and the removal of Khrushchev from power. However, the Soviets were struggling to maintain their lead in the space race. By 1967, it had been proven that humans could survive in space for long periods of time. It had also been proven that it was possible to dock a spacecraft and come back to Earth safely. The race was now on to see who could build a rocket with enough power to send a spacecraft to the Moon.

A rocket has to move with strong velocity to escape the Earth's gravity, but once in space, it can use less fuel. The Moon makes its own gravity that is about one-sixth as strong as the Earth's. This means that if a spacecraft can get close enough to the Moon, the craft will just fall toward it.

For a while, the Soviets continued with their lead in the space race. Although their chief designer Sergei Kovolev died in January 1966, the Soviets sent out a module called the *Luna 9*. The Soviets had sent probes before that had crash-landed on the Moon,

Luna *9 was the first spacecraft to safely land on the Moon and sent video and radio information about the Moon back to Earth.*

but the *Luna 9* set itself down gently on the Moon's surface.

Before the *Luna 9's* soft landing, no one knew the topography of the Moon's surface. The *Luna 9* proved that a craft could land safely on the Moon. Then, on March 31, the Soviets launched the *Luna 10*. The *Luna 10* actually made several orbits around the Moon over the course of 56 days.

The *Luna 9* and *Luna 10* missions were huge Soviet victories, but with Korolev gone, the Soviets had lost a genius who could not be replaced. Also, the Soviets simply could not enter into the next phase of rocket technology. In order to put people on the Moon, the rockets needed to be large enough to launch a space capsule that could hold astronauts or cosmonauts. Bigger rockets needed more effective fuel, and the Soviets could not yet make this happen.

In 1967, NASA scrapped the Redstone rockets they had been using and revealed the *Saturn V* rocket which had been designed by von Braun. The *Saturn V* used a three-stage fuel-injection process that sent rocket fuel to the thrusters.

The Soviets tried to keep up. They built the N-1

rocket, which was about the same size as the *Saturn V*, but it was not as efficient. The N-1 had first been thought of by Sergei Korolev before he died. Korolev knew how important rocket fuel was for planning a mission to the Moon. With a rocket as big as the N-1 the Soviets needed better fuel. NASA was creating rocket fuel made from a special kind of liquid hydrogen. The Soviets used a fuel made of liquid oxygen and kerosene, which was cheaper but less powerful.

The Soviets tested the N-1 rocket four times, and it blew up every time. The rocket was simply too big, and the building of its engine and fuel tanks were not properly designed for the rocket's size. After the introduction of the *Saturn V*, the United States was no longer racing against the Soviets. The US was now racing against JFK's deadline for putting a man on the Moon before 1970.

The summer Olympics of 1968 in Mexico City, Mexico highlighted additional inequalities separating Americans. Two African American track and field athletes named Tommie Smith and John Carlos both won medals in the 200-meter race. As

Tommie Smith and John Carlos' "Black Power" salute was one of many anti-racist protests. This moment became one of the most famous political moments in American sport history.

they stood on the podium, both Smith and Carlos raised their fists in a "Black Power" salute. It was a way of protesting unequal treatment for African Americans in the United States. The anti-war protest also grew louder and louder. While the Vietnam War seemed unwinnable, American troops continued to be sent overseas, upsetting many Americans.

After the disaster of the *Apollo 1* mission, NASA's engineers searched for mistakes they had made and set about fixing them. The next five Apollo missions tested the *Saturn V* rocket without using astronauts, and no one went into space at all for 21 months. It was October of 1968 before the scientists in NASA's Mission Control felt ready to put astronauts into space again. This was the *Apollo 7* space mission.

The goal of the *Apollo 7* was the same that it had been for *Apollo 1*. The craft was to be put into an orbit of the Earth while a new module was tested. This flight included one of the original seven Mercury astronauts, Wally Schirra. The mission was one of NASA's most flawless. It was time to start thinking about the Moon again. An *Apollo 8* mission went into planning.

For the *Apollo 8* mission, the goal was to have a spacecraft break free of Earth's gravity, fly all the way to the Moon, and then orbit the Moon before returning back to Earth. The *Apollo 8* mission was crewed by William A. Anders, Jim Lovell, and Frank Borman. It launched just four days before Christmas in 1968. The trip to the Moon took almost three days. Then, over the course of 20 hours, the *Apollo 8* orbited the Moon ten times. The crew was on television for Christmas Eve, which was seen and heard by upwards of one billion people.

Because the Moon rotates with the same side always facing the Earth, the *Apollo 8* astronauts were the first people to ever see the "dark side" of the Moon with their own eyes. They returned to Earth on December 27, 1968 when the *Apollo 8* spacecraft landed in the Pacific Ocean. There was nothing left for NASA to do but to prepare for a Moon landing, and the year 1969 was just about to begin.

Apollo 9 launched in March, but the goal of the mission was to test some technical equipment, especially a lunar module, while going into orbit around the Earth. The lunar module was the part of the spacecraft that would actually land on the Moon's surface.

The *Apollo 10* mission that followed was launched on May 18. The goal of the *Apollo 10* mission was to prepare directly for a Moon landing. The *Apollo 10* was supposed to do just about

Astronauts had to fit in the command module and be able to accomplish all of their tasks without getting frustrated with the small space or each other.

everything but actually land on the Moon. The *Apollo 10* orbited the Moon and then made an entry into the Moon's gravity and came just about eight miles from the Moon's surface before flying back to Earth. Neither Neil Armstrong nor Buzz Aldrin was aboard the *Apollo 10*. Instead, they were watching closely as they prepared for the *Apollo 11* mission that was set to launch before the end of 1969.

CHAPTER NINE

USA Wins the Space Race

By this time, the Soviet government had more or less given up on the space race against NASA. The US program was too far ahead now. Still, the Soviet space program continued to work to create an unmanned lunar probe that would land on the Moon without a cosmonaut.

As the end of the decade approached, many Americans began looking to NASA as a source of unity during very troubled political times. The *Apollo 11* mission was set to launch on July 16, 1969, and the goal was to have astronauts walking on the Moon by July 20 and returned safely to Earth soon after. In order to achieve this goal, the *Apollo 11* would have to contain both a command module and a lunar module.

The command module was shaped a bit like a Hershey's Kiss, and NASA had sent several into space. The command modules in the Apollo spacecrafts were some of the most complex machines ever created at the time. They included life support systems and technology for data collection. Most importantly, the command module took the astronauts into space then brought them back to Earth. This meant that the module had to be able to survive the fast and hot trip back to Earth. During reentry, incredible heat is created due to the force required to reenter Earth's atmosphere and the friction between the falling module and air particles.

The *Apollo 11* mission also had a lunar module, which was the vehicle that would take astronauts onto the Moon's surface. The lunar module would go into space, but it would not be coming home. Rather, the lunar module would be detached to reduce the weight of the landing gear. This ensured an easier lift off and trip home.

It may sound incredible, but the lunar module was covered in a metal foil not much thicker than

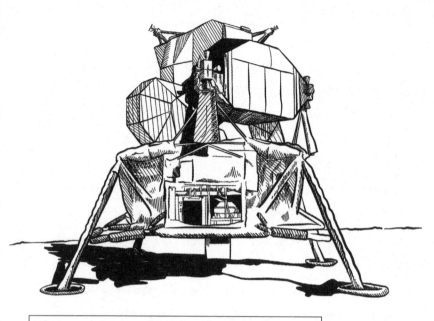

The lunar module served as the base of operations for everything the team would accomplish on the Moon's surface.

what you might wrap a sandwich in. The Moon has almost no atmosphere, so thick walls were not necessary. Thick walls would have only added weight. The lunar module would actually detach from the command module and then land two astronauts on the Moon.

The *Apollo 11* spacecraft was really three different vehicles. The *Saturn V* rocket would blast off into space carrying the command module (CM) and lunar module (LM). The rocket would then detach and fall away. The CM, with its own thrusters, would take the astronauts close to the Moon. Then the LM would detach from the CM and actually land on the Moon. After the astronauts explored, the LM would launch itself back onto the CM. The astronauts would then return home in the CM and leave the LM in space.

By July 16, NASA was set to launch the *Apollo 11* mission. Astronaut Michael Collins would pilot the CM, which was named *Columbia*. Astronauts Neil Armstrong and Buzz Aldrin were set to take the LM, called the *Eagle*, onto the Moon's surface. In training, Armstrong had gotten the reputation of being a daredevil. In 1968, he was in a lunar landing simulation that exploded seconds after his emergency evacuation. However, the process had prepared him well for the future Moon landing.

The mission began with all three astronauts sitting in the *Columbia* while it was attached to a *Saturn V* rocket. Millions of people watched on television as fire from the *Saturn V* rockets thrust the craft into the air. Television cameras rolled as the huge rocket seemed to take forever to fly into

Though not originally assigned to crew Apollo 11, *an assortment of delays and medical issues put the team of (left to right) Armstrong, Collins, and Aldrin together on the Moon.*

the sky, then the thrusters looked like a small spark, and then they disappeared from view. The three astronauts had left on their journey.

The *Saturn V* carried the astronauts into Earth's orbit and its engines stopped firing as planned. Earth's gravity then swung the *Apollo 11* around and launched the craft toward the Moon as the *Saturn V* started back up to provide enough thrust to send the *Apollo 11* in the right direction. From that point, the astronauts just had to settle in for a three-day ride to the Moon.

On July 19, the astronauts made it into the Moon's gravitational pull. The *Columbia* began to orbit the Moon with Michael Collins in control. Neil and Buzz put on their spacesuits, got on their

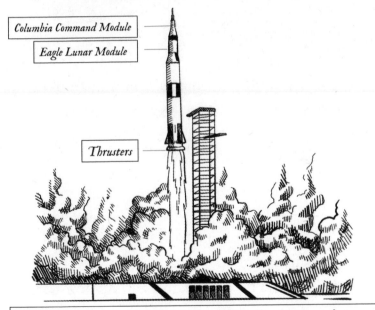

Columbia Command Module

Eagle Lunar Module

Thrusters

Roughly one million people watched the launch of Apollo 11 in person, but millions more around the world watched it on television. At the time, this was the most-watched TV event in history.

The computers used in the Apollo spacecrafts were unique for their time; they were small and portable.

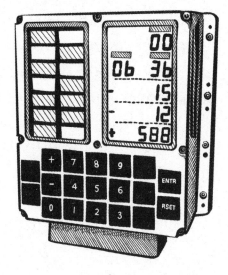

hands and knees, and crawled into the *Eagle* LM. With the two men inside, the *Eagle* was released from the CM and began to fall toward the Moon. The *Eagle* was equipped with radio and television transmitters, so even though Neil and Buzz were thousands of miles away from Earth, the world could watch and listen to them on the nightly news.

The Moon's surface is covered with rocks and craters, so finding a flat place to land was hard. NASA's team had decided to land the *Eagle* on a flat-looking surface named The Sea of Tranquility.

The *Eagle* had an engine and enough fuel to take it to a landing spot, but something was wrong. The *Eagle's* computer-based steering system was taking the astronauts right toward a massive crater. The astronauts could see that if they landed in that crater, then The *Eagle* would break apart. Armstrong turned off the computer and took control of the landing himself.

Armstrong and Aldrin would need to be careful since they needed enough fuel leftover in the tank if they were going to leave the lunar surface. Armstrong could not find a clear place to land and kept using up the engine's fuel. They were at fifty seconds, then forty seconds of fuel remaining.

Mission Control served as the Earth base for all communications with the astronauts and helped them tackle any problems that arose.

Armstrong would still not land. He was afraid of breaking the craft apart on the rocks. The fuel level continued to sink. Finally, Armstrong found a flat place and set the lunar module down. The engine had about thirty seconds of fuel left, just enough to blast off and dock with Michael Collins and the *Columbia*.

"Houston," Armstrong said through his radio, "the *Eagle* has landed."

In Houston, Texas, NASA's Mission Control engineers cheered. Then Armstrong dropped the exit ladder from the *Eagle* and stepped onto the Moon. Armstrong had prepared for this moment and he said, "That's one small step for [a] man,

While on the surface of the Moon, Armstrong and Aldrin performed a number of experiments and collected samples for scientists back on Earth to analyze.

Since the Moon doesn't have life or a strong atmosphere, there are no creatures or wind to erase Armstrong's footprints. They will be on the Moon forever.

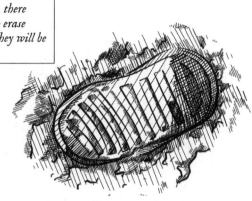

one giant leap for mankind." Neil Armstrong had become the first person to step onto the Moon. Buzz Aldrin quickly followed him, and the men spent over two hours exploring the Moon's surface. They planted an American flag, bounced around in the low-gravity, enjoyed the view, and collected a few rocks.

Once this was done, Neil and Buzz returned to the *Eagle*. The hardest part was still to come. The *Eagle* had to blast off the Moon and reconnect with the *Columbia*. They managed to do this, and with Neil and Buzz back on board, Michael Collins started the rocket engines, disconnected the lunar module, and the crew began the long trip back to Earth. The human dream of reaching the Moon had become reality.

CHAPTER TEN

The Future of Space Travel

On November 14, 1969, just a few months after the epic flight of *Apollo 11*, the *Apollo 12* went to the Moon. Astronauts Pete Conrad and Alan Bean stayed on the Moon's surface for a little over a full day before reconnecting with their command module and coming home. The US landed on the Moon twice more before the end of 1969. Americans thought that maybe Moon landings would become routine. Science fiction writers imagined that humans might live on the Moon and that space travel would become common for tourists.

Space travel, however, remained dangerous. Americans were reminded of this by the *Apollo*

13 mission that launched on April 11, 1970, with astronauts Jack Swigert, James Lovell, and Fred Haise on board. Given the success of the *Apollo 11* and *Apollo 12* launches, most people in the world thought that the *Apollo 13* would land safely on the Moon. It did not.

On April 13, Jack Swigert spoke words that were to become almost as famous as those said by Neil Armstrong. Swigert said "Houston, we've had a problem here." The problem was that the *Apollo 13* spacecraft was capable of producing much more power than previous crafts, but the cooling system was not strong enough to cool the generator down. In a complicated system like the spacecraft, it was hard to make all of the technologies compatible with each other.

An oxygen tank blew up fifty-six hours into the flight and tore a huge hole in one of the modules. At this point in the journey, the *Apollo 13* spacecraft was flying more than 200,000 miles away from Earth. The astronauts were safe in the command module, but they had nothing to eat or drink and oxygen would soon run out. The crew had to evacuate the command module and live in the lunar module, where they sat freezing and trying not to breathe up their oxygen supply. They had to use the lunar module's thrusters to power them into the Moon's orbit. The Moon's gravity then slung the *Apollo 13* spacecraft back toward Earth. Finally, on April 17, 1970, the *Apollo 13* crew landed safely in the Pacific Ocean.

The damage from the destroyed oxygen tank made a lunar landing impossible, so the astronauts abandoned the mission and returned to Earth.

The *Apollo 14* mission launched on January 31, 1971 and was notable for putting Alan Shepard, the first American in space, on the Moon. Neil Armstrong may have been the first man to step on the Moon, but Shepard was the first to play golf there. He hit a ball in the Moon's light gravity and jokingly bragged about how far it went.

The *Apollo 15* and *Apollo 16* missions were also successful, but by late 1972 it was not clear if continued missions to the Moon were worth the time and money. The last lunar landing occurred with the *Apollo 17* mission, launched on December 2, 1972 and featured a lunar rover which allowed astronaut Eugene Cernan to drive around on the surface. When the *Apollo 17* spacecraft returned home, NASA disbanded the Moon missions.

The Challenger missions of the 1980's were more inclusive than the Mercury, Gemini, and Apollo missions. Sally Ride became the first American woman to reach space in 1983 on the *Challenger 7* mission. Guion Bluford was the first African American to reach space on the *Challenger 8*.

Guion "Guy" Bluford became a NASA astronaut in 1979. After his forth and final flight, he logged more than 688 hours in space.

Then on January 28, 1986, the *Challenger 10* launched. This was an exciting launch that was supposed to attract a new generation of young people to space exploration. A high school social studies teacher named Christa McAuliffe was on board. The weather on that morning was below freezing, which was not normal for Cape Kennedy, Florida, the launch point. The cold weather affected the seals on the rocket booster. Just a few moments after the *Challenger 10* launched, it exploded in the air and killed all seven crew members. This tragedy occurred on millions of television sets in American homes and classrooms.

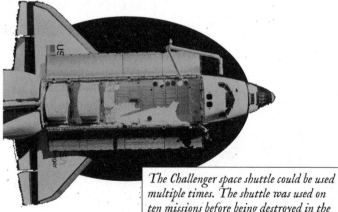

The Challenger space shuttle could be used multiple times. The shuttle was used on ten missions before being destroyed in the Challenger 10 *mission.*

In January of 2003, the space shuttle *Columbia* launched. In the first few minutes after takeoff, a piece of foam broke from a fuel tank and hit the left wing of the shuttle. Nothing went wrong until the *Columbia* returned from its space mission and reentered Earth's atmosphere. Then the small break in the left wing of the shuttle caused a series of problems that led to the *Columbia* breaking apart in the air. All seven crew members died in the explosion.

After the *Columbia* tragedy, NASA has had success with the *Atlantis*, *Discovery*, and *Endeavor* missions, but most of these missions occurred outside of the public eye. In November of 2011, NASA's space rover called *Curiosity* was launched all the way to Mars, where it landed safely and began sending back important data about the red planet. *Curiosity* is unmanned, so it showcases the technological and engineering skills of NASA's Mission Control rather than the impressive skills and courage of pilots. This, more than anything, is the difference between NASA now and NASA during the space race.

The first Moon landing of July 20, 1969 was something that brought America, and the world, together, if even for a short time. NASA's space shuttle was the single most expensive thing ever created. The shuttle represented the high point of engineering and technological achievement. Rocket technology that could have been used for a devastating war was instead used to reach new heights.

CHAPTER ELEVEN

SpaceX, NASA, and Mars

Today, when many hear about space travel and human space exploration, they think of Elon Musk and his company SpaceX, rather than NASA. This business man and wealthy investor uses his ever-evolving SpaceX company to increase space exploration and knowledge. He has talked about sending rockets and astronauts to Mars. However, this dream is very difficult to achieve.

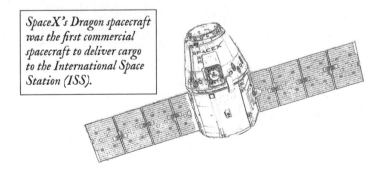

SpaceX's Dragon spacecraft was the first commercial spacecraft to deliver cargo to the International Space Station (ISS).

Even when Earth and Mars are at their closest point, a moment that only happens every 26 months, traveling takes a long time. For NASA's unmanned rover to reach the red planet, it took 253 days. NASA achieved manned missions of this length and longer, but only with the assistance of the International Space Station (ISS) where astronauts could restock on vital supplies. So, reaching Mars on a manned flight would require intensive planning to ensure the astronauts' safety.

For a round trip expedition to Mars, astronauts would be required to live in space for about two years. Due to the lack of long-term space travel, it is not clear

The International Space Station (ISS) is a home to astronauts and a place for science. It was created by many different countries and is a culmination of pieces. The first piece was launched in 1998 by Russia and many followed after. On November 2nd, 2000, two years after its start, the first crew arrived at the ISS.

how that would affect the mental and physical health of the astronauts.

Another problem would involve feeding the astronauts. The spacecraft would have to be equipped with the proper amount of food while also having ample storage for it. Typically, astronauts can stay for long periods on a space station, because they are not too far away from Earth. Unmanned rockets can be used to resupply space stations with vital items to ease life in space, such as oxygen, spare parts, and water. These rockets are also vital for sending back unnecessary items, like trash and dirty clothes. Without these rockets, long-term space travel would be difficult, uncomfortable, and dangerous.

Additionally, Mars lacks a magnetosphere. Earth's magnetosphere protects the living organisms (including humans) on our planet from dangerous levels of space radiation. Astronauts who landed on Mars would have to be protected at all times from the space radiation, and that would mean they would either have to live in protected capsules or immediately dig deep underground.

A manned expedition to Mars may be in the

distant future, but SpaceX and NASA are working to keep a new generation of Americans interested in rocket science and space travel. In recent years, NASA has launched two new projects that have captured the public's attention again. The first project is the James Webb space telescope and the second is the Artemis program.

The James Webb telescope is named after the first administrative head of NASA. It was created as a joint project with engineers from American, Canadian, and European space agencies. Building such a powerful telescope takes a lot of time and money, so the project was controversial. The telescope was supposed to cost one billion dollars and take eleven years to construct. Construction of the telescope began in 1996, and the first launch date was set for 2007.

However, the project ended up costing ten billion dollars and took more than two decades to construct. This caused a lot of controversy within NASA. The US Congress, which paid the bill, demanded answers about the extra costs and long delays.

However, the telescope did eventually launch in

December of 2021, and the images it produces of deep space are impressive. Generally speaking, the James Webb telescope is about six times more powerful than the Hubble telescope.

Given the overwhelming problems that come with sending humans to Mars, NASA will return to their original focus: the Moon. In 2017, NASA announced the Artemis Program which will include multiple missions to test new technologies and tools on the lunar surface. NASA plans to use their findings to help with their future goal of sending humans to Mars. This time, NASA has announced the intent of putting the first woman and the first person of color on the Moon's surface.

The Artemis program is a collaborative effort

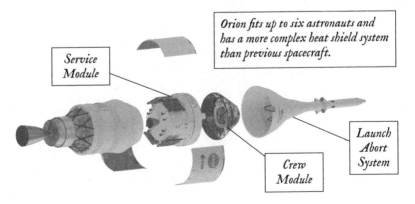

Orion fits up to six astronauts and has a more complex heat shield system than previous spacecraft.

Service Module

Crew Module

Launch Abort System

between twenty-one countries, including key US allies in Asia, Europe, and the Middle East. This time, NASA will draw upon engineers and technology that were developed by private companies.

Despite long delays, *Artemis 1* finally launched from NASA's Kennedy Space Station in Florida on November 16th, 2022. *Artemis 1* is the first test of new space explorations systems, including the Orion 1 spacecraft and Space Launch System (SLS) rocket. This vital test

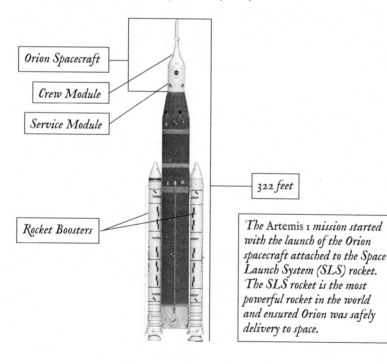

Orion Spacecraft

Crew Module

Service Module

322 feet

Rocket Boosters

The Artemis 1 *mission started with the launch of the Orion spacecraft attached to the Space Launch System (SLS) rocket. The SLS rocket is the most powerful rocket in the world and ensured Orion was safely delivery to space.*

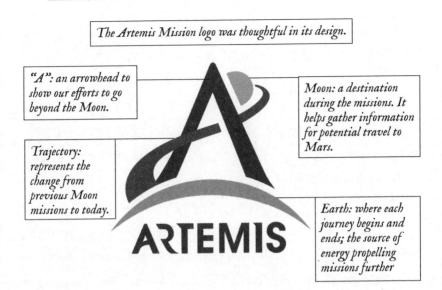

The *Artemis Mission* logo was thoughtful in its design.

"A": an arrowhead to show our efforts to go beyond the Moon.

Moon: a destination during the missions. It helps gather information for potential travel to Mars.

Trajectory: represents the change from previous Moon missions to today.

Earth: where each journey begins and ends; the source of energy propelling missions further

ARTEMIS

allows NASA to check their program before launching a full crew into space.

During countdown, the *Artemis 1* launch experienced a problem: there was a small hydrogen leak inside the mobile launcher. Although the Launch Control Center tried to fix the leak remotely at their base 4 miles away, they were unsuccessful. It was time to send in the red crew.

The red crew is a group of more than 40 people surrounding the launch base to fix any possible errors. To fix the hydrogen leak, NASA sent out crew members Billy Cairnes, Chad Garrett, and Trent Annis. They tightened bolts and double checked the valve, making sure the leak was fixed. They saved the launch, allowing the first Artemis mission to proceed successfully.

After nearly 26 days in space, the Orion spacecraft safely landed in the Pacific Ocean on December 11th, 2022. From its successful trip, NASA has received vital information to aid in the next Artemis missions and a gallery of updated images of the Moon and Earth.

Now, NASA is planning the *Artemis 2* mission. NASA astronauts Christina Hammock Koch, Reid Wiseman, and Victor Glover will join Canadian astronaut Jeremy Hansen on a journey around the Moon. Their mission is set to last ten days and is the next stepping stone in NASA's quest back to the Moon.

From JFK's speech in 1961 at Rice University to today, The United States' space program has achieved great milestones that were once thought to be impossible. NASA has sent astronauts to the Moon and rovers to Mars, all while collecting valuable data to help America learn more about space. The program has also developed new technologies that push our exploration further. Moving forward, Americans can expect great things from NASA and maybe even watch the first Mars landing come to fruition.

This is the President of the United States speaking. Through the marvels of scientific advance, my voice is coming to you from a satellite circling in outer space. My message is a simple one. Though this unique means, I convey to you and all mankind, America's wish for peace on Earth and good will to men everywhere.

President Dwight D. Eisenhower, 1958, speaking through an Atlas Satellite, the first spoken words transmitted through a satellite back to Earth

We choose to go to the Moon. We choose to go to the Moon in this decade and do the other things, not because they are easy, but because they are hard, because that goal will serve to organize and measure the best of our energies and skills, because that challenge is one that we are willing to accept, one we are unwilling to postpone, and one which we intend to win, and the others, too. It is for these reasons that I regard the decision last year to shift our efforts in space from low to high gear as among the most important decisions that will be made during my incumbency in the office of the Presidency.

President John F. Kennedy, 1962 speech at Rice University in Texas

It suddenly struck me that that tiny pea, pretty and blue, was the Earth. I put up my thumb and shut one eye, and my thumb blotted out the planet Earth. I didn't feel like a giant. I felt very, very small.

Neil Armstrong

Allied Countries: The 26 nations that signed the charter of the United Nations in 1945. This group fought against the Axis in WWII.

Astronautics: The science of spaceflight and travel.

Axis Countries: Germany, Italy, Japan, Bulgaria, Hungary, and Romania.

Civil Rights Act: Signed by President Lyndon B. Johnson in 1964; this banned the segregation of races in public places and made any discrimination based on race illegal.

Command Module (CM): The portion of a spacecraft that houses astronauts and keeps them on course. This piece returns astronauts to Earth.

Communism: A form of government characterized by a society where everything, including wealth, is divided among citizens; no one is allowed private land or money.

Cosmonaut: Term used for a Soviet space pilot; it is the Soviet equivalent of an American astronaut.

Dictator: A single person who holds absolute power.

Escape Velocity: This is the speed needed by an object to escape the gravitational pull of the planet it is on. For a rocket to leave Earth's gravity, it must be moving with enough thrust to "escape" the gravitational pull.

Fission Bomb: A bomb where energy is released by "splitting" the nucleus of an atom. Also known as atom bombs or nuclear bombs.

Fusion Bomb: A bomb where the fission process is used to create enough heat and pressure to "fuse" hydrogen into an isotope called deuterium. The Sun can be thought of as a giant fusion bomb. Also known as hydrogen or thermonuclear bombs.

Gravity: The force of a planet which draws objects towards its center, such as a planet keeping a human grounded.

Holocaust: The genocide of Jews and other minorities by the Nazis during WWII.

Hoosier: A native or resident of Indiana.

Lunar Module (LM): The portion of a spacecraft that releases from the command module and lands astronauts on the surface of the Moon.

Mission Control: An off-site center that monitors space missions. The team supports astronauts and keeps them safe.

Nuclear Energy: When nuclear energy is release quickly it creates an explosion; when released slowly it can be used to create electricity.

Operation Paperclip: A secret program authorized by the United States government to use about 1,600 former Nazi scientists to help develop the U.S. rocket program. Wernher von Braun was the most influential of these scientists.

Satellite: Any object that revolves around a larger object; example: the Moon is a satellite of Earth.

Soviet Union: Name for a coalition of fifteen countries that was dominated by Russia and the Communist Party. All fifteen countries stayed in the union from 1922-1956. Countries included: Armenia, Azerbaijan, Belarus, Estonia, Georgia, Kazakhstan, Kyrgyzstan, Latvia, Lithuania, Moldova, Russia, Tajikistan, Turkmenistan, Ukraine, and Uzbekistan.

Spacewalk: Term used for when a cosmonaut or astronaut leaves the spacecraft and floats in space.

Thrust: to push with force; the **thrusters** on a rocket push the vehicle upward

Transcontinental: Extending across a continent

Uranium: A highly radioactive element with an isotope that can be used to make nuclear weapons.

Velocity: The rate of how fast an object moves.

FDR: Franklin D. Roosevelt

JFK: John F. Kennedy

LBJ: Lyndon B. Johnson

MIT: Massachusetts Institute of Technology

NASA: National Aeronautics and Space Administration

CM: Command Module

ISS: International Space Station

LM: Lunar Module

RFK: Robert F. Kennedy

SLS: Space Launch System

WWI: World War One

WWII: World War Two

AUTHOR BIO

Chris Edwards, Ed.D, teaches world history, AP world history, and English at a public school in the Midwest. He is the author of numerous books on science, philosophy, and educational theory. He directs a summer institute for math and science teachers, is a frequent contributor to *Skeptic* magazine, and has presented his teaching methodology through publications and presentations with the National Council for Social Studies.

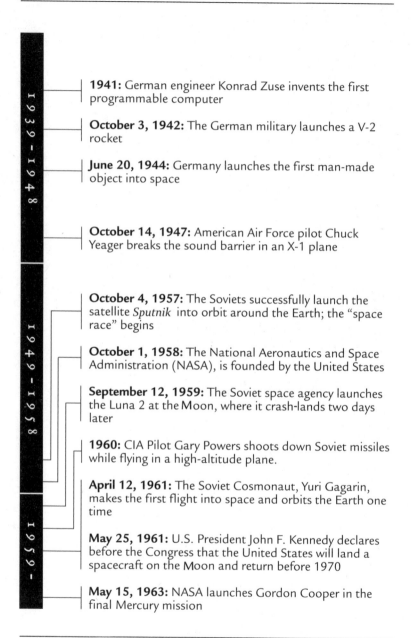

1939–1948

1941: German engineer Konrad Zuse invents the first programmable computer

October 3, 1942: The German military launches a V-2 rocket

June 20, 1944: Germany launches the first man-made object into space

October 14, 1947: American Air Force pilot Chuck Yeager breaks the sound barrier in an X-1 plane

1949–1958

October 4, 1957: The Soviets successfully launch the satellite *Sputnik* into orbit around the Earth; the "space race" begins

October 1, 1958: The National Aeronautics and Space Administration (NASA), is founded by the United States

September 12, 1959: The Soviet space agency launches the Luna 2 at the Moon, where it crash-lands two days later

1960: CIA Pilot Gary Powers shoots down Soviet missiles while flying in a high-altitude plane.

April 12, 1961: The Soviet Cosmonaut, Yuri Gagarin, makes the first flight into space and orbits the Earth one time

1959–

May 25, 1961: U.S. President John F. Kennedy declares before the Congress that the United States will land a spacecraft on the Moon and return before 1970

May 15, 1963: NASA launches Gordon Cooper in the final Mercury mission

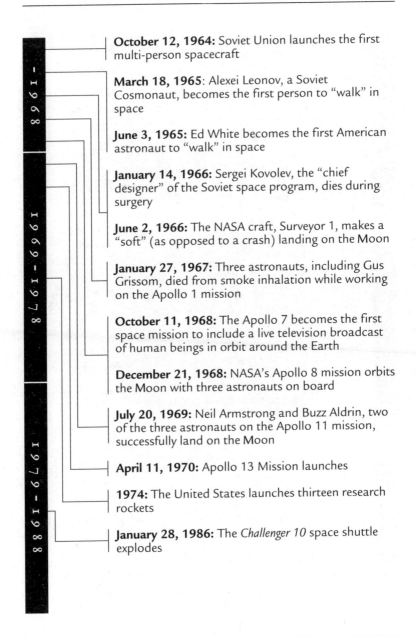

October 12, 1964: Soviet Union launches the first multi-person spacecraft

March 18, 1965: Alexei Leonov, a Soviet Cosmonaut, becomes the first person to "walk" in space

June 3, 1965: Ed White becomes the first American astronaut to "walk" in space

January 14, 1966: Sergei Kovolev, the "chief designer" of the Soviet space program, dies during surgery

June 2, 1966: The NASA craft, Surveyor 1, makes a "soft" (as opposed to a crash) landing on the Moon

January 27, 1967: Three astronauts, including Gus Grissom, died from smoke inhalation while working on the Apollo 1 mission

October 11, 1968: The Apollo 7 becomes the first space mission to include a live television broadcast of human beings in orbit around the Earth

December 21, 1968: NASA's Apollo 8 mission orbits the Moon with three astronauts on board

July 20, 1969: Neil Armstrong and Buzz Aldrin, two of the three astronauts on the Apollo 11 mission, successfully land on the Moon

April 11, 1970: Apollo 13 Mission launches

1974: The United States launches thirteen research rockets

January 28, 1986: The *Challenger 10* space shuttle explodes

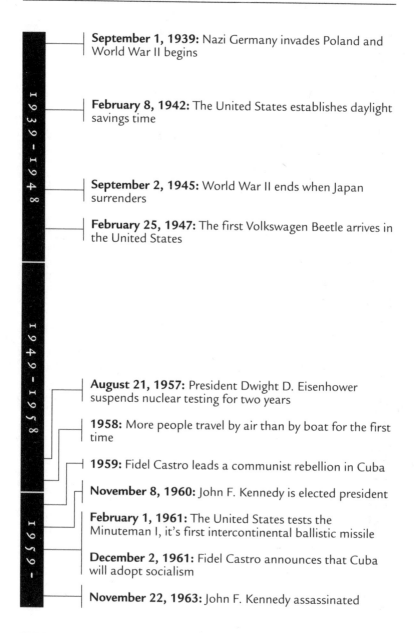

September 1, 1939: Nazi Germany invades Poland and World War II begins

February 8, 1942: The United States establishes daylight savings time

September 2, 1945: World War II ends when Japan surrenders

February 25, 1947: The first Volkswagen Beetle arrives in the United States

August 21, 1957: President Dwight D. Eisenhower suspends nuclear testing for two years

1958: More people travel by air than by boat for the first time

1959: Fidel Castro leads a communist rebellion in Cuba

November 8, 1960: John F. Kennedy is elected president

February 1, 1961: The United States tests the Minuteman I, it's first intercontinental ballistic missile

December 2, 1961: Fidel Castro announces that Cuba will adopt socialism

November 22, 1963: John F. Kennedy assassinated

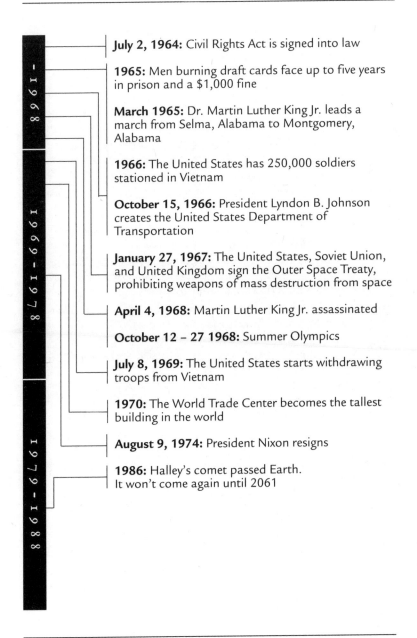

1968 - 1988

July 2, 1964: Civil Rights Act is signed into law

1965: Men burning draft cards face up to five years in prison and a $1,000 fine

March 1965: Dr. Martin Luther King Jr. leads a march from Selma, Alabama to Montgomery, Alabama

1966: The United States has 250,000 soldiers stationed in Vietnam

October 15, 1966: President Lyndon B. Johnson creates the United States Department of Transportation

January 27, 1967: The United States, Soviet Union, and United Kingdom sign the Outer Space Treaty, prohibiting weapons of mass destruction from space

April 4, 1968: Martin Luther King Jr. assassinated

October 12 – 27 1968: Summer Olympics

July 8, 1969: The United States starts withdrawing troops from Vietnam

1970: The World Trade Center becomes the tallest building in the world

August 9, 1974: President Nixon resigns

1986: Halley's comet passed Earth. It won't come again until 2061

REFERENCES

Burrows, William E. (1998). *This New Ocean: The Story of the First Space Age.* New York: Modern Library

Boomhower, Ray E. (2004). *Gus Grissom: The Last Astronaut.* Indianapolis: Indiana Historical Society.

Cadbury, Deborah. (2005). *Space Race: The Epic Battle Between America and the Soviet Union for Dominion of Space.* New York: Harper Perennial.

Jacobsen, Annie. (2014). *Operation Paperclip: The Secret Intelligence Program that Brought Nazi Scientists to America.* New York: Back Bay Books.

Kurson, Robert. (2018). *Rocket Men: The Daring Odyssey of Apollo 8 and the Astronauts Who Made Man's First Journey to the Moon.* New York: Random House.

Rhodes, Richard. (1995) *Dark Sun: The Making of the Hydrogen Bomb.* New York: Simon & Schuster.

Shetterly, Margo Lee. (2016). *Hidden Figures: The American Dream and the Untold Story of the Black Women Mathematicians Who Helped Win the Space Race.* New York: William Morrow.

Sparrow, Giles; John, Judith; McNab, Chris (editors). (2014). *The Illustrated History of Space Exploration: Discovering the Secrets of the Universe.* New York: Metro Books.

Wolfe, Tom. (2008). *The Right Stuff* (2nd ed.) New York: Picador.

FURTHER READING

Orr, Tamara. *All About Margaret Hamilton.* Indianapolis: Blue River Press, 2023.

Adamson, Thomas K. *The First Moon Landing (Graphic History).* Mankato: Capstone Press, 2006

Rocco, John. *How We Got to the Moon: The People, Technology, and Daring of Science Behind Humanity's Greatest Adventure.* Crown Books for Young Readers, 2020.

INDEX